THE

LITTLE LOCAL

NEW ORLEANS

COOKBOOK

THE
LITTLE LOCAL
NEW
ORLEANS
COOKBOOK

Recipes for Classic Dishes

STEPHANIE JANE CARTER

THE COUNTRYMAN PRESS
A division of W. W. Norton & Company
Independent Publishers Since 1923

For information about permission to reproduce selections
from this book, write to Permissions, The Countryman Press,
500 Fifth Avenue, New York, NY 10110

For information about special discounts for bulk purchases,
please contact W. W. Norton Special Sales at
specialsales@wwnorton.com or 800-233-4830

Manufacturing by Versa Press
Book design by Debbie Berne
Production manager: Devon Zahn

Library of Congress Cataloging-in-Publication Data

Names: Carter, Stephanie J., author. | Jentzen, Courtney, illustrator.
Title: The little local New Orleans cookbook / Stephanie Carter; illustrations
    by Courtney Jentzen.
Description: New York, NY : Countryman Press, [2019] | Includes index.
Identifiers: LCCN 2019006207 | ISBN 9781682684238 (hardcover)
Subjects: LCSH: Cooking, American—Louisiana style. | Cooking—
    Louisiana—New Orleans. | LCGFT: Cookbooks.
Classification: LCC TX715.2.L68 C373 2019 | DDC 641.59763/35—dc23
LC record available at https://lccn.loc.gov/2019006207

The Countryman Press
www.countrymanpress.com

A division of W. W. Norton & Company, Inc.
500 Fifth Avenue, New York, NY 10110

www.wwnorton.com

10 9 8 7 6 5 4 3 2 1

For Clementine

CONTENTS

Introduction 8

Drinks and Appetizers

Sazerac.. 12

Absinthe Frappé 13

Brandy Crusta 14

Ramos Gin Fizz.. 15

Hurricane... 16

Crabmeat Ravigote 17

New Orleans–Style Barbecue Shrimp..................................... 18

Soups, Sandwiches, and Sides

Creole Gumbo 22

Jim Core's Gumbo z'Herbs.. 25

Oyster Stew... 28

Yakamein 29

Crawfish Bread 32

Roast Beef Debris Po-Boy 34

Smothered Okra 37

Main Courses

Crawfish Étouffée 40

Chicken in Sauce Creole... 42

New Orleans–Style Seafood Boil 44
Chicken and Sausage Jambalaya 45
Blackened Redfish 48
Tailgate Shrimp Pasta 50
Red Beans and Rice 52

Eye Openers and Brunch
Brandy Milk Punch 56
Bloody Bull 57
Grits and Grillades 58
Eggs Sardou 61
Pain Perdu 64

Desserts
Bread Pudding 68
Bananas Foster 70
Pralines 72
King Cake 73
Calas 77

Acknowledgments 79
Index 80

INTRODUCTION

The streets of New Orleans are lined with friendly po-boy shops and tucked-away sno-ball stands; with historic bars proudly stirring up Sazeracs and flashy daiquiri shops that feature drive-thrus; with 150-year-old restaurants that serve flaming desserts tableside; with long oyster bars that make anyone who bellies up to them feel like a king; and with energetic culinary newcomers making waves every day. It's a wonderland with time measured in meals and celebrations.

Some say there are four seasons in Louisiana—crawfish, shrimp, oyster, and crab—but there are many more food seasons in New Orleans. The social life of the city revolves around these seasons, with denizens gathering to hunch over tables piled with crawfish, corn, potatoes, sausage, and rolls of paper towels for cleaning messy hands, or to down the gaily colored, sugary king cakes that anchor the revelry during Carnival season. There are seasons for okra, Creole tomatoes, and sno-balls, and many of Louisiana's iconic foods even have their own festivals. With contributions from the culinary traditions of African nations, Choctaw Indians, Haitians, Sicilians,

Germans, French, Croatians, and so many others, New Orleans' revered cuisine is built on giving everyone a turn at the pot. Considered the first true cuisine born in the United Sates, the Crescent City's foodways emerged from an exchange of ideas and flavors from various groups, all contributing to what we now consider to be Creole food. It's practically built into the definition of Creole food that, in New Orleans, food is an occasion for sharing and connection, one that all New Orleanians consider a part of who they are.

Ask a local where to get the best gumbo, and you'll hear "my mom's house" or "my grandmother's house." It's not helpful, but it's true. More than any other city in the United Sates, food is an identity here—one that all groups, regardless of race, class, social position, hold equally dear. As a result, New Orleans is a town where the home cook is alive and well. Often, the very best versions of classic New Orleans dishes are found in the home; indeed, some are *only* found there.

Consider this little cookbook an invitation to take your own turn at the pot.

DRINKS AND
APPETIZERS

SAZERAC

Makes 1 cocktail

In 2008, the Louisiana state legislature declared the Sazerac the official cocktail of New Orleans. This lightly sweet and spicy sipping cocktail should fill an old-fashioned glass just about halfway, a characteristic some say is the perfect expression of New Orleans optimism: The glass is always half full.

Ice cubes

1 4-gram sugar cube

4 dashes Peychaud's bitters

2 ounces Sazerac brand rye whiskey

¼ ounce Herbsaint liqueur

Garnish: fresh lemon peel
(about 2 inches long)

1 Fill an old-fashioned glass with ice. In a second glass, muddle together the sugar cube and bitters. Add the rye to the sugar and bitters and stir until the sugar dissolves.

2 Discard the ice from the first glass. Add the Herbsaint and swirl it around the interior walls of the glass. Discard the Herbsaint and pour the rye mixture into the Herbsaint-coated glass. Twist the lemon peel over the top of the drink to release some of its oils and serve.

Note: The original version of the Sazerac used absinthe.

ABSINTHE FRAPPÉ

Makes 1 cocktail

New Orleans' love affair with the Green Fairy stretches from when Oscar Wilde, Mark Twain, and other intellectuals sipped it at the Old Absinthe House. The absinthe frappé, created by Cayetano Ferrar at the Old Absinthe House in 1874, was *the* drink of the bohemian New Orleans culture of the late 1800s. Despite the dark days of Prohibition and the misguided absinthe ban, the Old Absinthe House soldiered on and still stands today, pouring absinthe frappés.

Crushed ice

8 to 10 fresh mint leaves, plus more for garnish

Ice cubes

1 ounce absinthe

½ ounce rich simple syrup (see Note)

1 egg white (optional)

1 ounce anisette, such as Marie Brizard (optional)

2 ounces club soda

1 Fill a glass with crushed ice.

2 Muddle the 8 to 10 mint leaves in the bottom of a cocktail shaker. Add the ice cubes, absinthe, and simple syrup. Add the egg white and anisette, if using. Shake vigorously. Strain into a glass and top with club soda. Garnish with extra mint leaves and serve.

Note: To make rich simple syrup, combine sugar and water in a 2:1 ratio (1 cup sugar to ½ cup water) in a saucepan over medium-low heat and cook, stirring constantly, until the sugar dissolves. Continue cooking for another 5 minutes. Remove from the heat and cool to room temperature.

BRANDY CRUSTA

Makes 1 cocktail

In 1850, when Italian bartender Joseph Santini concocted the first Brandy Crusta (named for the sparkling sugar crust around the rim of the glass) at the Exchange Hotel in New Orleans, he started a revolution. He was the first to add citrus to a cocktail, thus creating the first sour and a template for many well-known cocktails to come.

¼ cup granulated sugar

1 lemon wedge

1 whole lemon

1¾ ounces Cognac

¼ ounce maraschino liqueur

½ ounce orange liqueur, such as Grand Marnier or Cointreau

1 teaspoon simple syrup (see Note, page 13)

2 dashes Angostura bitters

Ice

1 Pour the granulated sugar onto a plate. Rub the rim of a pretty wineglass with the lemon wedge and immediately dip the wet rim into the granulated sugar. Set the glass aside so that the liquid dries and the sugar forms a sparkly crust.

2 Using a vegetable peeler or paring knife, remove the peel from the whole lemon in 1 long piece about 1 inch wide. Set aside.

3 Slice open the lemon and squeeze about 1 ½ tablespoons of juice from it. Add to a cocktail shaker.

4 Add the Cognac, maraschino and orange liqueurs, simple syrup, and bitters to the cocktail shaker and fill with ice. Shake and strain into the sugar-rimmed glass. Submerge the reserved lemon peel and serve.

RAMOS GIN FIZZ

Makes 1 cocktail

Henry C. Ramos created this silky, white, orange blossom-scented drink at New Orleans' Imperial Cabinet Saloon in 1888. By the end of the nineteenth century, the drink grew so popular that Ramos had to employ as many as three dozen "shaker boys" behind the bar at one time to shake the drinks. Eventually, Ramos sold his recipe to the Roosevelt Hotel, home of the Sazerac Bar, a favorite of Louisiana's gregarious longtime governor Huey P. Long. Long loved this ethereal cocktail so much that in 1935, he flew the Sazerac's head bartender to New York to coach bartenders there on the fine art of making it. He referred to it as his "gift to New York."

2 ounces dry gin

2 ounces heavy cream

1 large egg white

1½ ounces simple syrup (see Note, page 13)

½ ounce freshly squeezed lemon juice (juice of ½ lemon)

½ ounce freshly squeezed lime juice (juice of ½ lime)

1 teaspoon orange blossom water

Crushed ice

About 1 ounce club soda

In a cocktail shaker, combine all the ingredients except the crushed ice and club soda and shake hard until well combined, about 1 minute. Add the crushed ice to the shaker and shake for 1 minute more. Strain into a Collins glass (no ice) and top with the club soda until froth comes up over the rim of the glass like a cloud. Serve.

HURRICANE

Makes 1 cocktail

Pat O'Brien's, the famous French Quarter bar known for its hurricane cocktail, opened its doors two days *before* the end of Prohibition. It had in fact been preserving the Crescent City's drinking culture all along under a different name: Club Tipperary, which served bootlegged Caribbean rum throughout Prohibition and was open to anyone who knew the secret password, "storm's a brewin'."

When World War II created a whiskey shortage, liquor salesmen required bar owners to buy as much as fifty cases of less-desirable rum for just one case of Scotch. As a result, the cheery, sunset-hued rum-and-passionfruit Hurricane was born, with its name a reference to Pat O's Prohibition-era speakeasy password. This version is a reliably seductive summertime escape.

1 ounce dark rum

1 ounce light rum

1½ ounces passionfruit nectar

1 ounce orange juice

1 teaspoon grenadine

3 teaspoons simple syrup (see Note, page 13)

Ice cubes

Garnish: orange slice and maraschino cherry

Combine the rums, passionfruit nectar, orange juice, grenadine, and simple syrup in a cocktail shaker filled with ice. Shake and strain into a glass filled with ice. Garnish with the orange slice and cherry and serve.

CRABMEAT RAVIGOTE

Makes 8 servings

Among the most common cold appetizers on the Creole table, the New Orleans version of ravigote sauce is a cold, mayonnaise-based topper that's used to liven up fresh Louisiana jumbo lump crabmeat. You can stuff it into a hollowed-out tomato for a summer lunch; spoon it onto endive leaves or toast points for attractive hors d'oeuvres; or omit the seafood entirely and use the sauce as a dip with a whole grilled artichoke or crudité platter.

1 cup homemade or good-quality, store-bought mayonnaise, such as Blue Plate

1½ teaspoons Creole or deli-style mustard

3 teaspoons freshly squeezed lemon juice

2 tablespoons minced scallions

2 tablespoons minced red bell pepper

2 tablespoons minced anchovies

1 tablespoon minced capers

1 tablespoon minced fresh flat-leaf parsley

1½ teaspoons Worcestershire sauce

⅛ teaspoon freshly ground white pepper

Pinch of cayenne pepper

2 pounds jumbo lump crabmeat

1 In a medium bowl, combine the mayonnaise, mustard, lemon juice, scallions, red bell pepper, anchovies, capers, parsley, Worcestershire sauce, white pepper, and cayenne pepper.

2 Place the crabmeat in a large bowl and pour the sauce over it. Gently fold together the sauce and the crabmeat. Serve immediately or chill until serving.

NEW ORLEANS–STYLE BARBECUE SHRIMP

Makes 6 to 8 servings

To understand this dish, you must forget everything you know about barbecue. Throughout New Orleans, head-on Gulf shrimp get cooked with loads of butter, garlic, white wine, and Worcestershire sauce in a cast-iron pan. The dish arrives at the table with plenty of airy New Orleans–style French bread for sopping up all the butter sauce, but there's no smoke, no pit, and no barbecue sauce.

Pascal's Manale restaurant created the dish in the 1950s and keeps the original recipe under lock and key. The family, which has run the Creole-Italian restaurant for more than 100 years, even refused to share the recipe in its Pascal's Manale cookbook.

3 pounds Gulf shrimp, heads and tails intact (see Note)

2 cups shellfish stock (or 2 teaspoons Better Than Bouillon lobster stock base)

12 tablespoons (1½ sticks) unsalted butter

12 tablespoons (¾ cup) margarine

½ tablespoon minced garlic

½ cup vermouth

2 tablespoons freshly squeezed lemon juice

1½ tablespoons Worcestershire sauce

¼ teaspoon Hungarian sweet paprika

¼ teaspoon freshly ground black pepper

¼ teaspoon Italian seasoning blend

Pinch of cayenne pepper

½ teaspoon kosher salt

1 loaf New Orleans–style French bread, cut into ¾-inch-thick slices and toasted

1 Heat the oven on broil.

2 Peel the shrimp and remove the heads. Leave the tails intact. Refrigerate the shrimp.

3 Place the saucepan over medium heat and reduce the stock, if using, until it's thick enough to coat a spoon, about 30 minutes. Remove from the heat and let cool.

4 Pat the shrimp dry.

5 In a large cast-iron skillet over medium-low heat, melt 1 tablespoon of the butter. Add the garlic and sauté until cooked through. Increase the heat to high and add the vermouth and cook until the contents of the pan are nearly dry again. Add the reduced shrimp stock (or 2 teaspoons of Better than Bouillon lobster stock base), lemon juice, Worcestershire sauce, paprika, black pepper, Italian seasoning, cayenne, and salt. Reduce until the pan is nearly dry again. Whisk in the remaining butter and margarine. Add the shrimp and immediately remove from the heat.

6 Place the skillet under the broiler until the shrimp are cooked through, about 10 minutes, stirring once halfway through the broil time. Remove from the oven.

7 Serve in the skillet with the toasted French bread.

Note: Reportedly, margarine was part of the original recipe. It's still used today. If margarine seems too retro for you, substitute butter.

Note: The shrimp in this dish most often come head and shell-on. I like to use the heads and tails to make a stock first.

SOUPS, SANDWICHES, AND SIDES

CREOLE GUMBO

Makes 8 to 10 servings

More than a mere dish, gumbo is a religion. Each cook's unique take on gumbo has a tangible connection to the cooks who came before her, whether those sources are relatives or friends. Although dark-roux Cajun gumbos dominate contemporary menus, a lighter, more vegetable-rich gumbo brimming with seafood, tomatoes, and okra is the most traditional Creole version. To me, this is summertime gumbo that's perfect when okra and tomatoes reach their peak. Gumbo owes its name to the West African Bantu name for okra, *kingombo*. Although okra isn't found in all gumbos, the word "gumbo" gently reminds us of the great debt we owe to Africans for the South's rich culinary heritage.

FOR THE SHRIMP STOCK

3 pounds fresh Gulf shrimp, heads and tails intact and shells on

1 teaspoon peanut oil

¼ cup chopped carrot

¼ cup diced celery

½ cup diced onion

2 teaspoons tomato paste

½ cup dry vermouth, such as Noilly Prat

2 fresh flat-leaf parsley stems

1 fresh thyme sprig

1 whole clove garlic, unpeeled

1 bay leaf

5 black peppercorns

1 clove

FOR THE GUMBO

2 teaspoons kosher salt or to taste

½ cup plus 1 tablespoon peanut oil

4½ cups (about 3 pounds) fresh okra, sliced into ¼-inch-thick pieces

1 tablespoon unsalted butter

2 tablespoons all-purpose flour

1 cup finely diced white onion

1½ cups finely diced celery

1 cup finely diced green bell pepper

½ cup sliced scallions, plus more to garnish, white and green parts

2 cloves garlic, thinly sliced

4 cups very ripe chopped tomatoes with their juices

1 pound jumbo lump crabmeat

1 ham hock

½ tablespoon Worcestershire sauce, plus more as desired

1 bay leaf

Hot sauce as desired (optional)

5 cups cooked white rice for serving

Garnish: 1 bunch fresh flat-leaf parsley, chopped, and 2 bunches scallions, sliced

Make the shrimp stock:

1 Remove and reserve the heads and shells from the shrimp. Devein the shrimp and store in the refrigerator until ready to use in the gumbo.

2 In a 4-quart stockpot over high heat, warm 1 teaspoon of the peanut oil until very hot and a little vapor begins to rise. Immediately add the shrimp heads and shells and cook, stirring often with a wooden spoon, until pink, about 3 minutes. Add the carrot and cook, stirring often, for about 2 minutes. Repeat with ¼ cup of the celery.

3 Add ½ cup diced onion and sauté until translucent. Add the tomato paste and cook, stirring to coat, for about 1 minute.

4 Add the vermouth and cook, scraping the bottom of the pan to loosen any bits that have gotten stuck, until the pot is nearly dry, about 5 minutes. Add 3 quarts water and bring to a simmer.

5 Reduce the heat to medium-low and add all of the remaining stock ingredients, and simmer, uncovered, 1½ hours. Remove from the heat, strain through a fine mesh sieve, and discard the solids (this should yield 2 quarts stock). Set aside.

Make the gumbo:

1 In a heavy-bottomed skillet over high heat, warm ½ cup peanut oil until very hot. Add the okra and a dusting of salt and cook, stirring constantly, until the ropey texture disappears. The okra will stick, but just scrape the brown bits from the bottom. Remove from the heat and set aside.

2 In a 6-quart pot over medium heat, melt the butter with the remaining 1 tablespoon peanut oil. Make a roux by sprinkling the flour into the butter and oil and whisking until it is blended, cooked, and the color of a pecan.

3 Immediately add 1 cup diced onion and some of the salt and raise the heat to medium-high. Repeat with 1½ cups diced celery and bell pepper, each time adding more of the salt. Add the scallions and garlic and a little more of the salt and cook, occasionally stirring and scraping the bottom of the pan, for about 5 minutes.

4 Add the tomatoes and more of the salt and cook, stirring constantly, until the mixture nearly becomes a paste. Add the reserved okra and cook, stirring occasionally, for 1 minute more.

5 Reduce the heat to low and stir in ¼ of the crabmeat, reserving the rest. Add the reserved shrimp stock, 2 cups water, ham hock, Worcestershire sauce, bay leaf, and the remaining salt and simmer 1½ hours.

6 Add the reserved crabmeat and deveined shrimp and cook 30 minutes more, taking care that the mixture does not boil.

7 Remove and discard the bay leaf. Serve over hot rice and garnish.

JIM CORE'S GUMBO Z'HERBS

Makes 12 to 15 servings

New Orleans isn't known for vegetarian cuisine. Maybe that's because many cooks can't resist adding a little meat, even to vegetable dishes. Leftover ham hock? Throw it in! It'd be wasteful not to.

Consider gumbo z'herbs, otherwise known as green gumbo. This vegetarian gumbo was lauded during Lent and on other days that Roman Catholic tradition forbid the consumption of meat. But you'll be hard-pressed to find a truly vegetarian version. Gold standard-bearer Leah Chase of the New Orleans institution Dooky Chase only serves her gumbo z'herbs on Holy Thursday, and it includes multiple kinds of meat.

The recipe requires the cook to use at least seven different kinds of greens, but only in an odd number. The number of greens you use will predict the number of friends you'll make in the new year, so the more, the better.

This vegetarian recipe is from Jim Core, a beloved farmer who sold greens at the Crescent City Farmers Market for years. He cooked it for his wife, Gladys, who doesn't eat meat. Writer Sara Roahen included a version of it in a story she wrote for *Edible New Orleans*, a magazine I published and edited for several years.

Continued

¾ cup peanut oil

1 cup all-purpose flour

7 to 11 bunches different kinds of greens (collards, mustard greens, turnip greens, spinach, carrot tops, beet tops, arugula, parsley, scallions, watercress, any type of lettuce, curly endive, kale, radish tops, pepper grass), stems, cores, and discolored leaves removed and discarded

3 medium yellow onions, roughly chopped

½ head garlic, peeled

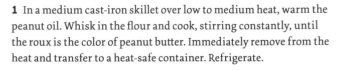

3 teaspoons dried thyme leaves

2 teaspoons ground cayenne pepper

3 bay leaves

Salt to taste

1 pound cooked red beans (canned is fine)

½ teaspoon filé powder (optional)

2 cups cooked white rice for serving

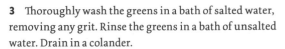

1 In a medium cast-iron skillet over low to medium heat, warm the peanut oil. Whisk in the flour and cook, stirring constantly, until the roux is the color of peanut butter. Immediately remove from the heat and transfer to a heat-safe container. Refrigerate.

2 Place a large stockpot filled with water over high heat and bring to a boil.

3 Thoroughly wash the greens in a bath of salted water, removing any grit. Rinse the greens in a bath of unsalted water. Drain in a colander.

4 Place half the greens, half the onions, and half the garlic in the boiling water. Reduce the heat to medium-low and simmer until the greens are very tender, about 20 minutes. Using a slotted spoon or colander with a long handle (do not drain the cooking water), transfer the cooked greens to a large bowl.

5 Return the same water to a boil and repeat with the remaining greens, onions, and garlic. If necessary, split the process into more than two batches. Remove from the heat and remove the final greens from the cooking liquid, reserving the liquid.

6 In batches, process the cooked greens, onion, and garlic in the bowl of a food processor fitted with the "S" blade or a meat grinder, adding reserved cooking liquid as necessary to reach a smooth consistency.

7 Add the pureed greens to a large stockpot over medium-high heat. Add more of the reserved cooking liquid until the texture is a medium-thick soup. Bring to a simmer and whisk in the chilled roux in batches, making sure that each application of roux is fully incorporated before adding more.

8 Add the thyme, cayenne, and bay leaves to the stockpot and continue simmering for about 1 hour, adding more cooking liquid if the mixture becomes too thick and reducing the heat as necessary to maintain a simmer.

9 Taste and season with the salt. Remove and discard the bay leaves. Stir in the red beans 5 minutes before serving. Serve the gumbo over rice with the filé powder on the table.

OYSTER STEW

Makes 8 servings

One of the most elegant classic New Orleans dishes also happens to be one of the easiest to make. This study in simplicity is perfect the way it is.

12 tablespoons (1½ sticks) unsalted butter

5 tablespoons all-purpose flour

1 large yellow onion, finely chopped

1 tablespoon kosher salt

4 celery stalks, finely chopped

4 cloves garlic, finely chopped

½ cup dry vermouth, such as Noilly Prat

¼ teaspoon finely ground white pepper

50 to 60 Gulf oysters, shucked and liquid reserved, or ½ gallon preshucked oysters and their liquid

2 cups whole milk

2 cups heavy cream

Garnish: chopped fresh flat-leaf parsley

1 In a 4-quart pot over medium heat, melt the butter. Add the flour and cook, whisking constantly, until the roux is golden. Add the onion and salt and cook until very soft. Repeat with the celery and then with the garlic. Add the vermouth and white pepper and cook until the pot is mostly dry.

2 Stir in the liquid from the oysters, milk, and cream. When the mixture begins to simmer, add the oysters and cook until their edges curl.

3 Ladle into bowls and top with the parsley. Serve immediately.

YAKAMEIN

Makes 8 to 10 servings

A mash-up of African-American and Asian cooking, some believe that yakamein sprung from the Chinese immigrants who arrived in the mid-nineteenth century to build railroads and work on sugar cane plantations. Another theory is that African-American soldiers got a taste of Asian food during the Korean War, brought it home, and adapted it to include local ingredients.

Nicknamed "Old Sober," this restorative broth brims with the umami saltiness of soy sauce and Creole seasoning; slippery strands of spaghetti; tender brisket; hard-boiled eggs; and chopped scallions. It's commonly served ladled into styrofoam cups from the back kitchens of bars and corner stores and alongside second line parades.

3 to 4 pounds boneless beef chuck roast, cut into 1-inch cubes

10 cloves garlic, halved lengthwise, plus 1 clove garlic, minced, divided

2 teaspoons kosher salt

¾ teaspoon freshly ground black pepper

4 tablespoons peanut oil

3 cups good-quality beef broth (I use Better Than Bouillon) plus 8 more cups

1 cup finely chopped yellow onion

3 teaspoons salt-free Creole seasoning blend, such as Tony Chachere's

½ cup finely chopped green bell pepper (about 1 pepper)

½ cup finely chopped celery stalk and leaves (about 2 ribs)

¼ cup thinly sliced scallions plus about ½ cup more for garnish

¼ cup chopped fresh flat-leaf parsley

¼ cup soy sauce

Continued

1 tablespoon Worcestershire sauce

1 tablespoon ketchup

1 pound angel hair pasta, cooked al dente according to package instructions

Garnish: 10 large hard-boiled eggs, hot sauce

1 Heat the oven to 300°.

2 With the tip of a paring knife, cut twenty 1-inch deep slits evenly over the roast and push the garlic pieces into the slits. Pat the roast dry and season it with 1 teaspoon salt and ½ teaspoon black pepper. Heat 2 tablespoons of oil in a large Dutch oven over high heat until it starts to shimmer. Brown the beef on all sides. Immediately add 3 cups of the beef broth so that it comes halfway up the roast. Cover tightly and place in the oven. Cook for 5 hours, spooning the broth over the meat about three times during cooking. Remove the meat from the broth and shred it with two forks. Discard the cooking liquid. Set the meat aside to cool or refrigerate overnight.

3 Heat the remaining 2 tablespoons of oil in a large stockpot over medium-high heat. When the oil appears to shimmer, add the onions, 1 teaspoon salt, ¼ teaspoon black pepper, and Creole seasoning. Sauté until the onion becomes soft and translucent. Repeat with the bell pepper followed by the celery and then by the garlic, each time cooking until softened. Add the ¼ cup scallions and the parsley. Cook, stirring constantly, 1 minute. Add the soy sauce, Worcestershire sauce, and ketchup and cook, stirring constantly, 1 to 2 minutes more.

4 Raise the heat to high and add the reserved meat, remaining 8 cups of broth, and 1 cup water. Bring to a boil.

5 Reduce the heat to medium-low and simmer uncovered for 30 minutes. Remove from the heat.

6 Divide the cooked pasta among 8 bowls (about ¼ cup each). Ladle the meat and broth over it. Slice the hard-boiled eggs in half lengthwise and top each portion of soup with two halves of hard-boiled egg and sprinkle with more of the scallions. Serve with the hot sauce on the side.

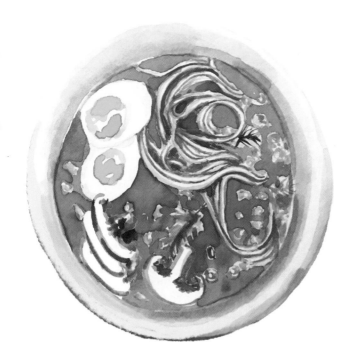

CRAWFISH BREAD

Makes eight 3-inch servings

Although the Crescent City already overflows with classic dishes, new ones are constantly joining the canon. About twenty-five years ago, John Laborde of Avoyelles Parish was making a school lunch lady's sausage bread recipe and, on a whim, switched out the sausage for crawfish and adjusted the seasonings. His new dish earned him a coveted vendor spot at the New Orleans Jazz Fest, and decades later, the crawfish bread booth still draws some of the longest lines each year. This is my version of his classic.

2 tablespoons unsalted butter

2 tablespoons olive oil

3 teaspoons coarse kosher salt, plus more as needed

1 cup finely diced yellow onion (about 1 medium onion)

½ cup finely diced red bell pepper (about 1 pepper)

½ cup finely diced celery (2 to 3 stalks)

6 cloves garlic, minced

½ cup dry vermouth, such as Noilly Prat, or dry white wine

1 pound Louisiana crawfish tails and their liquid

1 teaspoon Hungarian sweet paprika

½ teaspoon dry mustard

⅛ teaspoon freshly ground black pepper

¾ cup scallions, thinly sliced, light green and white parts only (about 1 large bunch)

6 tablespoons mayonnaise

1 cup shredded mozzarella

1 cup shredded mild Cheddar

Freshly squeezed juice of ¼ lemon

2 20-inch loaves soft French or Italian bread

1 In a large sauté pan over medium-high heat, melt together the butter and oil. Add the onion, followed by the bell pepper, and then the celery. Add about 1 teaspoon salt (this does not need to be exact) and sauté until the vegetables wilt, about 5 minutes (the bell pepper will lend some of its color to the onion, which will be otherwise translucent). Stir in 1 teaspoon salt. Add the garlic and cook until that, too, is translucent, about 2 minutes.

2 Add the vermouth and reduce until the pan is nearly dry and the vermouth no longer smells acidic.

3 Reduce the heat to medium and add the crawfish and their liquid. Cook, stirring to combine, about 2 minutes. Add the paprika, dry mustard, the remaining 1 teaspoon salt, and a grind of black pepper and stir until well combined. Remove from the heat.

4 Stir in the scallions and mayonnaise. Stir in ⅓ cup each mozzarella and Cheddar until just combined. (You will use the rest of each during assembly.) Add the lemon juice, taste, and season with more salt and black pepper, if necessary. Refrigerate overnight.

5 Heat the oven to 400°F.

6 Split open each loaf of bread and scoop out some of the soft interior with your hands. Sprinkle about a quarter of the remaining cheeses on the bottom part of each loaf. Spread ½ the chilled filling over the cheese on each loaf. Top with the remaining cheese.

7 Close the bread so that it looks like a long sandwich. Place the loaves on a baking sheet and bake until the filling is warm and the cheese melts. Remove from the oven, slice, and serve.

Note: If you want to cook these ahead of time, wrap them in foil and keep them warm in the oven.

ROAST BEEF
DEBRIS PO-BOY

Makes five 6-inch sandwiches

The iconic po-boy came about as a result of a contentious streetcar strike in 1929. In 1922, Bennie and Clovis Martin left their jobs as streetcar conductors and opened the Martin Brothers' Coffee Stand in the French Market. The brothers sympathized with the strikers and promised free sandwiches—usually light and airy New Orleans French bread filled with fried potatoes or roast beef debris—to any hungry striker. In a letter of support, they wrote, "We are with you 'til hell freezes, and when it does, we will furnish blankets to keep you warm." When a hungry striker came in for his sandwich, they'd call out, "Here comes another poor boy!"

1 3- to 4-pound boneless beef chuck roast

10 cloves garlic, halved lengthwise

1 teaspoon kosher salt

½ teaspoon freshly ground black pepper

2 tablespoons peanut oil

About 3 cups high-quality low-sodium beef broth, plus more if needed

3 12-inch loaves New Orleans po-boy bread (substitute inexpensive soft French bread from the grocery store if necessary)

Mayonnaise as needed (optional)

Garnish: Thinly sliced tomatoes, thinly sliced dill pickles, and thinly shredded iceberg lettuce (optional)

Sliced cheese (optional)

Louisiana hot sauce (optional)

Ketchup (optional)

1 Heat the oven to 300°F.

2 Using the tip of a paring knife, evenly cut twenty 1-inch deep slits all over the roast and push the garlic pieces into them. Pat the roast dry and season with the salt and black pepper.

3 In a 6-quart Dutch oven over high heat, warm the vegetable oil until it starts to smoke. Add the beef and sear on all sides, being sure to get it very brown.

4 Immediately add the 2 cups beef broth so that it comes halfway up the roast (add more if necessary). Cover, place in the oven, and roast 5 hours, basting the meat with the broth several times during cooking. Remove from the oven and shred the meat with two forks. Refrigerate the meat and its cooking liquid together overnight.

5 In a large pot over medium heat, heat the meat, its cooking liquid, and a cup of water. Cook, stirring frequently, until it resembles a meaty gravy.

6 Cut the loaves open lengthwise and spread the mayonnaise in the interior of each.

7 Cover the bottom half of each loaf with the tomato slices and pickles, if using, and spoon the roast beef and gravy over it. Top with sliced cheese (if using) and the shredded lettuce (if using). Close the sandwich and slice in two. Serve immediately.

Note: If you'd like to make a French fry po-boy, cover the bottom half of each loaf with cooked and lightly salted French fries and spoon the roast beef and gravy over that. Top with sliced cheese (if using). Dress as desired with the tomatoes, pickles, and lettuce. Close the sandwich, slice in two, and serve immediately.

TO MAKE A SHRIMP PO-BOY

Toss 3 pounds of shrimp in a cup of all-purpose flour. Remove the shrimp from the flour and shake off any excess. Add the flour-coated shrimp to a mixture of 3 beaten eggs and two tablespoons of water. Remove the shrimp from the egg mixture. Toss the shrimp in a mixture of 1 cup of all-purpose flour, 1 cup of fine cornmeal, 2 teaspoons of kosher salt, and a tablespoon of Creole seasoning. Shake off excess seasoning. Heat about 6 cups peanut or vegetable oil to 360°F in a large pot. Add the shrimp, working in batches as necessary, and fry until golden brown and crispy, about three minutes per batch. Split the bread lengthwise, add mayonnaise, hot sauce, ketchup, shredded iceberg lettuce, sliced tomatoes, and sliced dill pickles.

Note: Can't decide between the roast beef debris or the shrimp? Add them both to the same po-boy and you've got a Peacemaker po-boy.

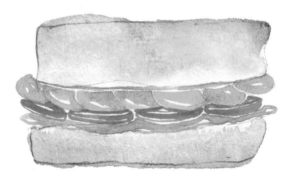

SMOTHERED OKRA

Makes 8 servings as a side dish

There's probably no vegetable more emblematic of Southern identity than okra. Brought to the American South by African slaves, okra crops flourished in southern climes. Here's a great dish for using the summer okra harvest that freezes well.

3 pounds fresh okra, sliced into ½-inch rounds (about 10 cups sliced)

¼ cup bacon fat or other oil

2½ teaspoons kosher salt

½ teaspoon freshly ground black pepper

Pinch of cayenne pepper

1 cup chopped onion

½ cup chopped celery

½ cup chopped bell pepper

5 cloves garlic, minced

3 cups diced tomatoes and their juices

1 cup chicken or vegetable stock

1 Pat the okra dry. In a 4-quart cast-iron pan over high heat, warm the bacon fat. Add the okra, a third of the salt, the black pepper, and the cayenne pepper. Reduce the heat to medium and sauté until the okra is brown and the slime is gone.

2 Add the onion, celery, bell pepper, garlic, and another third of the salt and sauté until the vegetables are soft. Add the tomatoes and their juices, the stock, and the rest of the salt.

3 Reduce the heat to low and cook, covered but stirring occasionally, until the okra is tender, about 1 hour. Remove from the heat and serve hot.

MAIN COURSES

CRAWFISH ÉTOUFFÉE

Makes 4 servings

Louisiana's crawfish farms are in Acadiana, as are the roots of this dish. After farmers harvest their rice, they flood the fields and use them to farm crawfish, which eat what's left of the decaying rice plants, thus naturally preparing the field for the next rice planting. While the fields are flooded, duck hunting season opens, and hunters set up in the flooded fields to hunt the ducks that fly over them.

If you can't get Louisiana crawfish (more commonly available crawfish from China lack flavor), substitute small shrimp. This recipe was inspired by Rima and Richard Collin's indispensable *The New Orleans Cookbook*, published in 1975.

6 tablespoons (¾ stick) unsalted butter

¼ cup all-purpose flour

1 cup finely chopped white onion

½ cup finely chopped green bell pepper

½ cup finely chopped celery

1 tablespoon minced garlic

2 teaspoons kosher salt

1 pound crawfish tails with fat (see Note)

⅓ cup thinly sliced scallions, white and green parts, plus more for serving

1 tablespoon minced fresh flat-leaf parsley

1 teaspoon freshly squeezed lemon juice

¼ teaspoon freshly ground black pepper

⅛ teaspoon ground cayenne pepper

2 cups cooked white rice for serving

1 In a large, heavy-bottomed 5-quart pot over low heat, melt the butter. Gradually whisk in the flour, stirring constantly until fully incorporated. Continue stirring until the roux turns medium-brown, about 20 minutes.

2 In this order, add the onion, bell pepper, celery, garlic, and half the salt, cooking each until its softened before adding the next. Stir and cook until the vegetables are coated and very soft, about 20 minutes. Add the crawfish tails and their fat, the remaining salt, the scallions, parsley, lemon juice, black pepper, and cayenne pepper and mix thoroughly.

3 Raise the heat to medium, add 2 cups water, and simmer for about an hour or until the étouffée forms a gravy thick enough to coat the back of a spoon. Adjust the seasoning to taste. Keep warm until you're ready to serve. Serve hot over the rice and top with additional scallions.

Note: This dish gets better if it sits in the refrigerator overnight. Just reheat it over low heat, adding more water if it becomes too thick.

Note: You can find crawfish tails in their own fat in the freezer section of some grocery stores.

CHICKEN IN SAUCE CREOLE

Makes 8 servings

While most people have heard of shrimp Creole, chicken cooked in the same sauce is also popular. It also bears similarities to the Haitian dish *Poulet a L'Haitienne*, or *Poule en Sauce*, which many consider to be the ancestor of New Orleans' sauce Creole. In Haitian culture, it is common for a dish to have several names depending on which part of the country from which a cook hails.

3 pounds chicken breast, cut into 1-inch pieces

1 teaspoon plus 1 teaspoon kosher salt

½ teaspoon plus ¼ teaspoon freshly ground black pepper

3 tablespoons peanut oil

4 tablespoons (½ stick) unsalted butter

2 cups finely chopped onions

1 cup finely chopped green bell pepper

1 cup finely chopped celery

1 tablespoon minced garlic

1 tablespoon salt-free Creole seasoning mix, like Tony Cachere's

Pinch of ground cayenne pepper

3 ounces (½ can) tomato paste

2 tablespoons all-purpose flour

⅓ cup dry vermouth, such as Noilly Prat

1 14.5-ounce can diced tomatoes in their juices

2 cups chicken stock

1 bay leaf

1 teaspoon Worcestershire sauce

1 teaspoon hot sauce

½ cup chopped scallions

2 tablespoons chopped fresh flat-leaf parsley, plus more for garnish

4 cups cooked white rice for serving

1 Rinse the chicken and pat it dry. Season it with 1 teaspoon salt and ½ teaspoon black pepper.

2 In a large heavy pot over medium-high heat, warm the peanut oil. Add the chicken pieces, leaving a little space between each, and brown about 3 minutes on each side. Remove the chicken and set aside on a paper towel–lined plate. (The chicken does not need to be fully cooked at this point.)

3 In the same skillet over medium heat, melt the butter. In this order, add the onions, green bell pepper, celery, and garlic, cooking each until it begins to soften before adding the next. Add the remaining 1 teaspoon salt and ¼ teaspoon black pepper, the Creole seasoning mix, and the cayenne pepper and cook, stirring constantly, until the vegetables wilt, about 8 minutes.

4 Add the tomato paste, stir to combine, and cook until it smells sweet, about 2 minutes. Sprinkle in the flour and cook, stirring constantly, until the vegetables are fully coated, about 1 minute. Add the vermouth and simmer until most of the vermouth is cooked away. Add the tomatoes and juices, chicken stock, bay leaf, Worcestershire sauce, and hot sauce. Increase the heat to high and bring to a boil. Add the reserved chicken and reduce the heat to low.

5 Cover and simmer 20 minutes, stirring occasionally to prevent the sauce from sticking to the bottom of the pot.

6 Remove the lid and simmer until the sauce thickens, another 20 minutes. Stir in the ½ cup scallions and 2 tablespoons parsley. Taste and adjust the seasoning. Remove from the heat and remove and discard the bay leaves.

7 Divide the rice among 8 dishes and top each with the chicken and sauce. Garnish with additional parsley and serve immediately.

NEW ORLEANS–STYLE SEAFOOD BOIL

Makes 4 to 5 servings

From spring to early summer, New Orleans social life revolves around backyard seafood boils, where friends gather around long, newspaper-covered tables to peel shrimp or crawfish and wash it all down with cold beer.

1 gallon water or broth

½ cup dry vermouth

1 onion, roughly chopped

3 stalks celery, cut into 2-inch pieces

½ head garlic, peeled

1 lemon, sliced

1 pound smoked sausage, such as andouille (about 2 links)

2 tablespoons kosher salt

3 tablespoons cayenne pepper

½ teaspoon black peppercorns

2 bay leaves

½ pound 2-inch new potatoes (or other waxy variety), halved

2 ears fresh corn, shucked and sliced in thirds

2 pounds whole shrimp (or crawfish, crabs, or a combination)

1 In large stockpot over high heat, bring the water to a boil. Add the vermouth, onions, celery, garlic, lemon slices, sausage, salt, cayenne pepper, black peppercorns, and bay leaves and return to a boil. Boil until all the vegetables are soft, about 20 minutes. Add the potatoes and boil until the potatoes are nearly soft, about 10 minutes. Add the corn and boil 3 minutes more.

2 Reduce the heat to low, add the whole shrimp, and simmer until the shrimp is cooked through, about 10 minutes. Remove from the heat. Strain and discard the liquid from the pot. Serve the shrimp immediately.

CHICKEN AND SAUSAGE JAMBALAYA

Makes 12 servings

New Orleanians adopted jambalaya from the Cajuns, who make brown jambalaya, a dish that typically includes chicken and sausage. Red jambalaya, which is made with tomatoes and often includes shrimp and ham, is considered the definitive Creole version. Both kinds are popular throughout the city, with many variations in between. This one-pot rice dish is great for using up leftovers, so it's a go-to for home cooks. In fact, it's difficult to find it in restaurants at all.

4 strips bacon, finely diced

4 tablespoons peanut oil, plus more as needed

2½ pounds white and dark meat chicken, rinsed and cut into 1-inch pieces (see Note)

2 teaspoons kosher salt

1 teaspoon freshly ground black pepper

½ teaspoon plus ⅛ teaspoon salt-free Creole seasoning mix, like Tony Cachere's

1 pound andouille sausage, cut into ¼-inch rounds

2½ cups finely diced white onions (about 2 onions)

1½ cups finely diced celery (about 4 stalks)

1½ cups finely diced green bell peppers (about 2 bell peppers)

8 cloves garlic, minced

1 teaspoon Worcestershire sauce

1 teaspoon Louisiana hot sauce, such as Tabasco

Pinch of cayenne pepper

1 28-ounce can diced tomatoes and their juices

3 cups uncooked long-grain white rice

5 cups chicken stock

Garnish: 1 cup thinly sliced scallions and ½ cup minced fresh flat-leaf parsley

Continued

1 In a heavy, 7- to 8-quart pot over medium heat, fry the bacon until crisp and bubbling. In a colander set over a bowl, strain the fat from the bacon. Reserve the bacon fat. Set the bacon aside to drain on paper towels. Carefully wipe the pot clean with a paper towel.

2 Pat dry the pieces of chicken and season with half the salt, half the black pepper, and ½ teaspoon Creole seasoning.

3 Heat the reserved bacon fat and peanut oil in the pot over medium-high heat. Working in batches as necessary, brown the chicken parts on all sides. (The chicken does not have to be fully cooked at this point.) Remove the cooked pieces to a paper towel–lined platter.

4 Add the sausage to the hot oil, adding more oil if necessary, and saute for 2 minutes. In this order, add the onions, celery, bell pepper, garlic, and the rest of the salt, pepper, and Creole seasoning and cook until they become soft and translucent, stirring and scraping the bottom of the pot as you go, about 5 minutes.

5 Add the Worcestershire sauce, Tabasco sauce, and cayenne pepper and cook 1 minute more. Add the tomatoes and their juice and cook until the mixture parts and comes together slowly when you draw a wooden spoon through it, 20 to 30 minutes. Return the chicken and bacon to the pot, followed by the rice. Stir until the rice is coated.

6 Add the stock, stirring and scraping any particles off the bottom of the pan. Raise the heat to high and bring to a boil.

7 Stir one more time, reduce the heat to low, cover, and cook 20 minutes. Remove from the heat and let stand, covered and undisturbed, 15 minutes.

8 Uncover and fluff the rice with a fork. Fold in the parsley and scallions and serve.

BLACKENED REDFISH

Makes 6 servings

In the 1980s, when Paul Prudhomme created blackened redfish at his no-frills restaurant K-Paul's, the dish became so feverishly popular that redfish fishing had to be regulated. Outside Louisiana, the frenzy ignited interest in Cajun cuisine. Today, blackening is common all over the world, but the sublime original walks a tightrope few have mastered, as the spices never overwhelm the palate with heat. This recipe is adapted from Prudhomme's own.

1 tablespoon sweet Hungarian paprika

2½ teaspoons kosher salt

1 teaspoon onion powder

1 teaspoon garlic powder

¾ teaspoon cayenne pepper

¾ teaspoon freshly ground black pepper

¾ teaspoon freshly ground white pepper

½ teaspoon dried thyme leaves

½ teaspoon dried oregano leaves

1 tablespoon minced fresh Italian parsley

¾ pound (3 sticks) unsalted butter

6 skinless redfish (or other firm-fleshed fish) fillets, each about ½ inch thick (see Note)

Lemon slices for serving (optional)

1 Thoroughly combine the paprika, salt, onion powder, garlic powder, cayenne pepper, black pepper, white pepper, thyme, and oregano in a small bowl. Set aside.

2 Place 2 sticks of the butter in a small pot over medium-low heat. Heat until the butter bubbles and the milk solids rise to the top.

Continue cooking until the milk solids fall to the bottom and it stops bubbling. Pour the clarified butter through a filter and strainer into a bowl, trying to leave behind as much of the solid matter as possible. Set aside. Melt the remaining stick of butter.

3 Pour 2 tablespoons of the melted butter each in four small ramekins and set aside and keep warm. (I usually keep them next to the stove.) Pour the remaining butter in a shallow bowl and keep warm.

4 Turn the exhaust fan on high. Open the doors or windows in the kitchen. Heat a large cast-iron skillet over high heat for about 10 minutes.

5 While it heats, submerge each redfish fillet in the large bowl of butter until fully coated on all sides. Generously sprinkle the spice mixture and parsley over one side of the fish. Repeat with the other side.

6 Carefully place the fillet in the hot pan, the side that never had skin down and with space between each. Quickly top each with 1 tablespoon butter and sauté the first side until charred. Flip over the fish and pour 1 teaspoon butter over it. Transfer to a plate and repeat until all the fish is cooked. Serve immediately with the ramekins of butter.

Note: Tuna makes an excellent substitute for the redfish, one Prudhomme himself used after the redfish ban was in place. You can also substitute chicken for the fish; finish in a 350°F oven if necessary.

TAILGATE SHRIMP PASTA

Makes 6 servings

Whether you're a football fan or not, it isn't hard to fall in love with LSU tailgates, filled with everything from Bloody Mary bars to buffets often overflowing with specialties like grillades and grits and this rich, creamy, and lightly spicy seafood pasta, a version of which also appears on the table at family and community gatherings throughout New Orleans. You can substitute crawfish for the shrimp.

2 teaspoons kosher salt, plus more for pasta water

1 pound short pasta, such as penne or rotini

1 teaspoon extra virgin olive oil

4 tablespoons (½ stick) unsalted butter

2 cloves garlic, minced

¼ cup finely chopped yellow onion

¼ cup finely chopped scallions

Pinch of freshly ground black pepper

5 teaspoons salt-free Creole seasoning, like Tony Chachere's

¼ cup brandy

2 pounds small to medium shrimp, peeled and deveined

2 cups heavy cream

Juice of ½ lemon

½ pound jumbo lump crabmeat (optional)

1 Bring a large pot of heavily salted water (it should taste like seawater) to a boil over high heat. Add the pasta and cook according to package instructions until al dente. Drain, reserving 1 cup of the pasta water. Cool the pasta in an ice bath and drain again. Toss the cooled pasta with the olive oil to prevent sticking. Set it aside. Rinse the pasta pot and wipe it clean and dry.

2 In the pasta pot over medium-high heat, melt the butter. Add the garlic and sauté until it starts to turn gold and smell toasty, about a minute. Quickly add the onion and a third of the salt, and cook until soft and translucent. Add the scallions and stir until combined. Add another third of salt, the black pepper, and the Creole seasoning and raise the heat to high. Add the brandy, stir to combine, and cook until you no longer smell the alcohol in the brandy, 2 or 3 minutes.

3 Reduce the heat to medium-low and add the reserved pasta water. Whisk in the cream. Simmer, stirring and scraping the sides of the pot often, until the mixture thickly coats the back of a spoon. It will appear thick, but the shrimp will leach water and loosen it. Add the shrimp, remaining salt, and cook until the shrimp turn pink and curl. Add the pasta and stir until evenly coated and warmed through. Squeeze the lemon juice over the pot and stir again.

4 Stir in the lump crabmeat (if using), turn off the heat, and cover the pot. Let it sit, covered, for 8 minutes. Uncover and serve immediately.

RED BEANS AND RICE

Makes 6 servings

In New Orleans, nothing cures the Monday blues better than red beans and rice. A tradition of eating red beans on Mondays grew out of a different Monday tradition, washing the laundry. The meal didn't need any tending to, and it could sit on the same hot coals used to heat the wash water. Sunday's leftover ham bone could be thrown in for seasoning.

New Orleans school cafeterias—private, public, or parochial—serve this dish for lunch on Mondays, usually with a side of cornbread and a vegetable. It's a hearty, flavorful meal that's economical, easy, and perfect for feeding a crowd.

3 tablespoons bacon fat or other oil

2 cups finely chopped white onions

½ cup finely chopped green bell pepper

2 tablespoons minced garlic

½ cup thinly sliced scallions, plus more for garnish

2 tablespoons minced fresh flat-leaf parsley, plus more for garnish

2 pounds dried red beans soaked overnight in cold water and drained

½ pound pickled pork, cut into 1-inch pieces

1 smoked ham bone meat still attached

2 teaspoons kosher salt, plus more to taste

½ teaspoon freshly ground black pepper

Pinch of cayenne pepper

2 bay leaves

Cooked white rice for serving

Hot sauce for serving

1 In a large, heavy 8- to 10-quart pot over medium heat, warm the bacon fat. Add the onions and cook until translucent. Add the bell pepper and cook until soft. Repeat with the garlic. Add the scallions and parsley and cook 1 minute more.

2 Add the drained beans, pickled pork, ham bone, and enough cold water to cover by 3 inches. Add the black pepper, bay leaves, and cayenne pepper.

3 Reduce the heat to low, offset the pan a bit on the burner, and simmer, partially covered, for at least 6 hours, stirring every 30 minutes. Add more hot water if the beans get too dry. The beans are ready when a thick gravy has formed and the beans are soft. Add the salt to taste and remove from the heat.

4 Remove and discard the ham bone and bay leaves. With the back of a spoon, mash some of the beans against the side of the pot so that the entire mixture is creamier.

5 Ladle the beans and gravy over the hot rice, top with parsley and scallions, and serve with hot sauce on the side.

EYE OPENERS AND BRUNCH

BRANDY MILK PUNCH

Makes 1 cocktail

Eggs and booze are part of New Orleans' DNA. After all, brunch was first popularized here at Madame Begue's, where it was called "second breakfast" and served as a sort of nightcap for dock workers. When the 1884 World's Fair arrived in town, the masses discovered second breakfast, renamed it brunch, and took the concept home with them. Later, Commander's Palace invented the jazz brunch.

Brunch is a sacred ritual and a lingering affair that necessarily involves booze. Otherwise, it's just breakfast. Sweet, creamy, stomach-coating brandy milk punch is a brunch standard in New Orleans.

Ice cubes

2 ounces brandy

4 ounces half-and-half

1 ounce simple syrup
(see Note, page 13)

¼ ounce vanilla extract

Garnish: freshly grated nutmeg

In a cocktail shaker filled with ice, combine the brandy, half-and-half, simple syrup, and vanilla extract. Shake until very cold. Strain into a pretty glass filled with ice, garnish with the nutmeg, and serve.

Note: This is an easy recipe to make your own. Switch out the brandy for rum. Add a teaspoon or two of crème de menthe or banana liqueur for extra flavor. It's also an easy recipe to prepare in a big batch, as I like to do for Christmas morning.

BLOODY BULL

Makes 1 cocktail

From the original tomato-juice-and-vodka version to ones involving clam juice to those that are garnished with wacky stuff like cheeseburgers and bacon, nearly everyone has a version of the Bloody Mary. In the 1950s, French Quarter restaurant Brennan's subtle addition—a splash of Campbell's beef broth—added umami depth to garden variety Bloody Marys. Pickled green beans are the garnish of choice in New Orleans.

2 ounces vodka

4 ounces tomato juice

4 ounces Campbell's beef broth, unconstituted

2 teaspoons freshly squeezed lemon juice

4 dashes Tabasco or other hot sauce

2 dashes Worcestershire sauce

About ½ teaspoon freshly grated horseradish

Pinch of freshly grated black pepper

Pinch of celery salt

Ice cubes

Garnish: pickled green beans and/or pickled okra (optional)

In a cocktail shaker, combine the vodka, tomato juice, beef broth, lemon juice, Tabasco sauce, Worcestershire sauce, horseradish, black pepper, celery salt, and Creole seasoning. Add ice and shake well. Fill a glass with ice and strain the Bloody Mary into it. Garnish and serve.

GRITS AND GRILLADES

Makes about 5 servings

Shrimp and grits reigns as the South's most famous grits preparation, and New Orleans restaurants serve many excellent versions. But you'll have to thank South Carolina's Low Country for that dish, which arrived in New Orleans when it arrived just about everywhere else. New Orleans has its own grits dish, made with tender veal cooked in a rich, swamp-dark gravy. If you haven't heard of it, there's a good reason: The most celebrated versions come from home cooks.

2 teaspoons plus one teaspoon kosher salt

½ teaspoon freshly ground black pepper

¼ teaspoon ground cayenne pepper

1 cup all-purpose flour

2 pounds boneless veal or beef round steak, cut into 3-inch pieces and pounded to ⅛-inch thickness

3 to 6 tablespoons bacon fat, shortening, lard, or peanut oil

1½ cups finely diced yellow onion (about 1 large onion)

1 cup finely diced celery

1 cup finely diced red bell pepper (about 2 bell peppers)

1 teaspoon minced garlic

½ cup sliced scallions, white and green parts (about 1 bunch)

½ cup dry red wine

¼ cup dry sherry

1½ cups diced tomatoes in their juices

3 bay leaves

2 teaspoons Worcestershire sauce

1 teaspoon Tabasco or other hot sauce

2 cups good-quality beef stock

1 cup white or yellow grits

2 tablespoons unsalted butter

Garnish: 1 bunch scallions, thinly sliced

1 Heat the oven to 375°F.

2 In a small bowl, combine 2 teaspoons salt, the black pepper, and the cayenne pepper. Place the flour in a large bowl.

3 Pat the meat dry. Sprinkle the spice and salt mixture evenly on all sides of the meat pieces and then dredge them in the flour. Shake off any excess flour.

4 In a large Dutch oven over medium heat, warm the 3 tablespoons of bacon fat. Brown the meat on each side until the meat doesn't stick when you flip it, about 2 minutes per side. Add more fat to the pan if the bottom of the pot becomes too dry. Remove the meat to a paper towel–lined plate.

5 In order, immediately add the onion followed by the celery, bell pepper, garlic, scallions, and 1 teaspoon of salt to the pan, waiting for each to soften slightly before adding the next and stirring constantly with a wooden spoon. Stir and cook until the vegetables wilt. Add the red wine and sherry, stir and scrape the fond from the bottom of the pan, and reduce until both have evaporated, about 2 minutes. Add the tomatoes with their juices, bay leaves, Worcestershire sauce, and hot sauce and cook 10 minutes more. Reduce the heat to low and add the beef stock.

6 Return the meat to the pot, making sure it's covered with the sauce. Cover, place in the oven, and cook 1 hour. Remove from the oven and place it back on the burner over low heat. Uncover and reduce until the sauce thickens, about 5 minutes. Remove from the heat and take out and discard the bay leaves.

7 In a large pot over high heat, bring 5 cups of water to a boil. While whisking constantly, scatter the grits into the boiling water.

Continued

8 Reduce the heat to medium-low and cook, whisking constantly (the constant whisking keeps them from clumping and agitates the starch so they become creamy), until the grits are very soft, about 30 minutes. If too thick, add more hot water as needed. Once thickened and soft, whisk in the remaining 2 tablespoons salt and the butter.

9 Place the meat and gravy over the grits, garnish with the scallions, and serve.

EGGS SARDOU

Makes 8 servings

By 1930, Antoine's restaurant already had 560 egg recipes. Many, like this one, have become brunch classics. The dish is named for the French playwright Victorien Sardou, who's best known for writing *La Tosca*, the play on which Puccini based his opera. What most people think of as classic eggs Sardou isn't Antoine's recipe at all. Brennan's added creamed spinach to the dish, but Antoine's piles up artichoke bottoms with a couple anchovies, a poached egg, and hollandaise—and then rains diced ham and shaved truffles over all that.

FOR THE CREAMED SPINACH

2½ teaspoons plus 2 tablespoons unsalted butter, divided

⅛ cup finely diced yellow onion

1 teaspoon kosher salt, plus more as needed

¾ tablespoon all-purpose flour

½ cup whole milk

¼ cup heavy cream

1 bay leaf

1 black peppercorn

1 whole clove

Pinch of freshly grated nutmeg

¼ cup Gruyère or white Cheddar

2 tablespoons unsalted butter

2 tablespoons finely chopped shallot

1 pound frozen spinach, thawed, drained, and squeezed dry

¼ teaspoon freshly ground black pepper

FOR THE HOLLANDAISE SAUCE

¼ cup white wine vinegar

1 tablespoon finely chopped shallot

½ teaspoon cracked black peppercorns

4 large egg yolks

¾ pound (3 sticks) unsalted butter, melted and kept warm

2 teaspoons freshly squeezed lemon juice

Continued

Pinch of ground cayenne pepper

Kosher salt to taste

2 tablespoons white vinegar

1 tablespoon kosher salt

8 whole large eggs

8 artichoke bottoms, warmed

Garnish: chopped fresh flat-leaf parsley and finely diced ham, and shaved truffles (optional)

Make the creamed spinach:

1 In a medium saucepan set over medium-low heat, melt 2½ teaspoons butter. Add the onion and cook, stirring occasionally, 2 to 3 minutes. Sprinkle in the flour and cook about 3 minutes. Whisk in the milk and cream.

2 Raise the heat to medium and bring the mixture to a simmer. Add the bay leaf, peppercorn, and clove and cook, stirring occasionally, at the barest simmer until the sauce coats the back of a spoon, about 20 minutes (be careful that the milk and cream do not scorch). Strain, discarding the solids, and mix in the cheese. Set aside.

3 In a large sauté pan over medium heat, melt 2 tablespoons butter. Add 2 tablespoons shallot and a pinch of salt. Cook, stirring occasionally, until translucent, 2 to 3 minutes. Add the spinach and more salt. Cook, stirring occasionally, until the spinach is warm and most of the liquid has steamed away.

4 Remove from the heat and stir in the cream sauce. Taste and add more salt and a grind of black pepper if necessary.

Make the hollandaise sauce:

1 Fill a pot with about 2 inches of water and bring to a simmer over medium heat.

2 In a small pan over medium heat, combine the vinegar, 1 tablespoon shallot, and black peppercorns and reduce until the pan is nearly dry. Add 2 tablespoons water to the reduction and strain into a stainless-steel bowl that fits over the pot containing the simmering water.

3 Add the egg yolks to the bowl and set the bowl into the pot of simmering water (it's important that the bowl does not touch the water). Gently cook, whisking constantly, until the sauce thickens into a ribbon-like consistency.

4 Remove the bowl from the simmering pot of water and pour the warm butter into the bowl in a thin stream while whisking constantly. Add up to 2 tablespoons water if the butter does not fully absorb. Blend in the lemon juice, salt, and cayenne pepper. Set aside.

Make the eggs:

1 Bring a large pot of water to a boil.

2 Reduce the heat to medium, leaving the water at a bare simmer. Add the vinegar and salt.

3 Break each egg into a clean cup. As you stir the simmering water in a circular fashion so it spins on its own, slide each egg, one at a time, into the spinning water. Cook until the whites are set and opaque, about 3 minutes. Remove with a slotted spoon.

Assemble the dish:

Divide the 8 warm artichoke bottoms among 4 plates. Top each artichoke with the creamed spinach and 1 poached egg. Crown with the hollandaise sauce. Garnish with the parsley and the chopped ham and add the truffles, if using. Serve.

PAIN PERDU

Makes 4 servings

Many cultures make a version of French toast or eggy bread. In New Orleans, it's known as pain perdu, literally "lost bread." The main difference in New Orleans is that we usually use the local version of French bread, which is the airy, thin-crusted bread used for po-boys, rather than the denser breads most French toast recipes use. Reviving it with what amounts to a crème brûlée base is certainly a good excuse for buying bread for no reason other than to let it get stale.

8 large egg yolks

1¾ cups half-and-half

¼ cup granulated sugar

2 tablespoons orange blossom water

½ teaspoon vanilla extract

10 to 15 ¾-inch-thick slices day-old French Bread (preferably New Orleans–style)

3 tablespoons unsalted butter

3 tablespoons vegetable oil (or any neutral flavored oil)

Confectioners' sugar for dusting (optional)

Louisiana cane syrup for drizzling (optional)

1 Heat the oven to 200°F. If the bread hasn't fully dried, toast in the oven for about 10 minutes, flipping once.

2 In a large mixing bowl, whisk together the egg yolks, half-and-half, sugar, orange blossom water, and vanilla extract until the custard is smooth and silky. Place as many bread slices in the custard that can fit in a single layer in your nonstick skillet until soaked through, about 20 seconds per side.

3 Warm a nonstick skillet over medium heat. Add 1 tablespoon butter and 1 tablespoon oil to form a light coating on the bottom of the pan. Add the soaked bread slices and cook, flipping once, until the bread is golden brown on each side, 4 to 5 minutes. (If the custard spreads when it touches the pan, raise the heat a notch so that the custard cooks before it has time to spread.)

4 Wipe clean the pan and repeat the process until you've cooked all the bread.

5 Dust with confectioners' sugar or drizzle with the cane syrup before serving, if desired. Serve immediately or place on a baking sheet in the warm oven until ready to serve.

Note: Substitute any flavoring you like for the orange blossom water, such as brandy or Grand Marnier.

DESSERTS

BREAD PUDDING

Makes 8 to 10 servings

Like Pain Perdu (page 64), this recipe elevates stale bread by soaking it in a mixture of eggs, cream, and sugar before it's baked and laced with whiskey sauce. Whether it's made with stale bread or not, it's a piece of cake to eat like a king in New Orleans. Served warm with the whiskey sauce, bread pudding makes a decadent dessert. Without the sauce, it pairs well with morning coffee.

FOR THE BREAD PUDDING

1 30-inch loaf New Orleans–style French bread, torn into small pieces (about 16 cups)

2 cups whole milk

3 cups heavy cream

1 vanilla bean

4 large eggs plus 6 large egg yolks, beaten

1 cup granulated sugar

6 tablespoons (¾ stick) salted butter, cubed

Scalding water, as needed

FOR THE WHISKEY SAUCE

½ cup granulated sugar

1/16 teaspoon kosher salt

2½ cups heavy cream

1 cup bourbon or other whiskey

2 tablespoons cornstarch

2 tablespoons unsalted butter

Make the bread pudding:

1 Heat the oven to 300°F.

2 Place the bread pieces in a single layer on a sheet pan and place in the oven until the bread is fully dried, about 10 minutes.

3 In a medium saucepan over medium-low heat, warm the milk, 3 cups cream, and 1 cup sugar, taking care not to scald the milk. When the mixture begins to simmer, slice the vanilla bean lengthwise and scrape the seeds into the milk mixture. Add the pod as well, remove the pot from the heat. Cover and steep at least 10 minutes. Remove the pods, scraping any remaining seeds into the saucepan.

4 Once the cream and milk mixture has nearly cooled to room temperature, pour it in a thin stream into the eggs, whisking constantly.

5 In a 9-by-13-inch casserole dish, arrange half the bread in a layer and pour half the milk and egg mixture evenly over it. Press it gently so that the bread becomes saturated. Repeat with the remaining bread and liquid. Refrigerate 5 hours or overnight.

6 Heat the oven to 300° F. Evenly scatter the salted butter cubes over the top.

7 Place the casserole dish inside a larger dish with tall sides. Fill the larger dish halfway with scalding water, making a water bath to keep the bottom and sides from browning. Cover with foil and bake 1 hour. Uncover and bake until the top is golden and the bread pudding no longer wiggles, about an hour more. Remove from the oven and let the bread pudding rest for 15 minutes before serving.

Make the whiskey sauce:

1 In a small saucepan over medium heat, combine ½ cup sugar, salt, and 2½ cups cream, stirring constantly. In a separate bowl, whisk together the bourbon and cornstarch. Whisk the bourbon mixture into the cream mixture and increase the heat to high to bring it to a boil. Immediately remove it from the heat and stir in the butter.

2 Drizzle over the warm bread pudding and serve immediately. (Bring any extra sauce to the table in a sauce boat.)

BANANAS FOSTER

Makes 4 servings

In the 1950s, the New Orleans port along the Mississippi River brought in lots and lots of bananas from Central and South America. A surplus of these inexpensive yellow beauties led to a stroke of genius in the kitchen of the French Quarter's Brennan's restaurant: One of New Orleans' most iconic desserts, Bananas Foster, was born. It's brilliantly simple, really—bananas are sliced lengthwise and flambéed tableside in dark rum, banana liqueur, sugar, and cinnamon, and the mixture is spooned hot over vanilla ice cream.

Vanilla ice cream for serving (1 generous scoop per person)

4 ripe bananas

½ cup dark brown sugar, densely packed

4 tablespoons (½ stick) unsalted butter

¼ cup banana liqueur

¼ cup aged rum

½ teaspoon ground cinnamon

1 Scoop the ice cream into four bowls and set aside in the freezer until the sauce is complete.

2 Peel the bananas and slice lengthwise, then in half. Set aside.

3 In a medium pan over medium heat, combine the sugar and butter and cook until the sugar is dissolved. As the butter melts, add the banana liqueur and stir to combine.

4 Add the bananas to the pan and continue to cook, turning once, until the bananas start to soften and brown, about 3 minutes per side.

5 Raise the heat to medium-high and add the rum. Once the rum is heated, ignite it using a long lighter or shake the pan back and forth over a gas flame until it ignites. Agitate it a bit to keep the flame going and sprinkle the cinnamon into the flames. The cinnamon will look like sparks as it flames. Remove from the heat.

6 Divide the banana pieces and sauce among the four bowls of ice cream. Serve immediately.

PRALINES

Makes 25 pralines

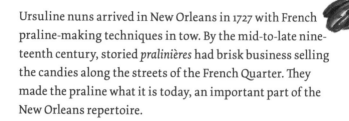

Ursuline nuns arrived in New Orleans in 1727 with French praline-making techniques in tow. By the mid-to-late nineteenth century, storied *pralinières* had brisk business selling the candies along the streets of the French Quarter. They made the praline what it is today, an important part of the New Orleans repertoire.

1½ cups pecan halves

¾ cup granulated white sugar

1½ cups dark brown sugar, densely packed

½ cup whole milk

¼ teaspoon kosher salt

1 teaspoon vanilla extract

6 tablespoons (¾ stick) unsalted butter

1 Line a baking sheet with parchment paper. Mash pecan halves so that you have halves, pieces, and powder.

2 In a medium, heavy pot over low to medium-low heat, combine everything except the pecans. Cook, stirring constantly with a wooden spoon, until the sugar dissolves and the mixture becomes bubbly and reaches the soft ball consistency, about 238°F on a candy thermometer. Remove from the heat and immediately stir in the pecan halves, pieces, and powder. Mix vigorously until the mixture thickens and becomes cloudy. The pecans will no longer sink at this point.

3 Using a kitchen tablespoon, quickly start dropping generous spoonfuls of the mixture onto the parchment-lined baking sheet, leaving about 3 inches between each spoonful. Let cool 2 hours.

KING CAKE

Makes 2 large king cakes

This Mardi Gras classic officially hits New Orleans bakeries on Twelfth Night, which marks the opening of Carnival season. That's the first moment it's acceptable to eat king cake. Since Twelfth Night falls on January 6, it also means that any New Year's resolutions involving weight loss are out of the question. If you're lucky enough to get the king cake baby, know that it is both a gift and a mandate: It's up to you to bring the king cake to the next party, which is probably tomorrow. If you can't get a plastic baby, stuff the cake with a single dried fava bean, which was the norm until the late 1800s.

1½ tablespoons active dry yeast

1 tablespoon plus ⅓ cup granulated sugar

¼ cup warm water (about the temperature of bath water)

5 to 6 cups all-purpose flour

1¼ cups plus 3 tablespoons warm whole milk

2 whole large eggs, room temperature

3 large egg yolks room temperature

1 tablespoon finely grated orange zest

2 teaspoons kosher salt

1 teaspoon ground cinnamon

½ teaspoon plus ¼ teaspoon vanilla extract

¼ teaspoon almond extract

12 tablespoons (1½ sticks) European-style unsalted butter, diced and at room temperature

4 tablespoons (½ stick) unsalted butter, melted (optional)

1 tablespoon ground cardamom (optional) (see Note)

⅛ cup granulated sugar (optional)

1 tablespoon heavy cream

2 cups confectioners' sugar

2 tablespoons light corn syrup

3 cups coarse white sugar

Red, blue, and yellow food coloring (see Note)

Continued

1 Dissolve the yeast and 1 tablespoon of sugar in the warm water. Let it stand until it becomes foamy, about 15 minutes. In the bowl of a stand mixer fitted with the paddle attachment, combine the yeast mixture, 2 cups flour, and 1¼ cups milk. Beat on medium-high for about 1 minute, scraping the sides of the bowl as necessary, until the mixture is smooth.

2 Add 1 cup flour, 1/3 cup sugar, the whole eggs, 2 egg yolks, the orange zest, the salt, the cinnamon, ½ teaspoon vanilla extract, and the almond extract to the mixing bowl and beat on medium with the paddle attachment until smooth.

3 Add 12 tablespoons butter a little at a time, fully incorporating each bit before adding more. Repeat until all the butter is added.

4 While the mixer is running, add 2 cups flour, ¼ cup at a time, fully incorporating each bit before adding more. There should be 1 cup flour remaining; slowly add this flour, a little at a time, and continue beating just until the dough comes together and the walls of the bowl are clean (you may not need the full 1 cup to achieve this).

5 Place the dough on a floured work surface and knead until smooth and soft, about 4 minutes. If the dough sticks while you're kneading it, add a little flour.

6 Transfer the dough to a large, greased bowl. Roll the dough around in it until coated in oil. Cover with plastic wrap and set aside at room temperature until doubled in size, about 2 hours.

7 Press down the dough to deflate it. Cover and refrigerate overnight.

8 Press down the dough again to deflate it. On a floured work surface, split the dough into 2 equal pieces and roll each out until it is about a quarter of an inch thick. Try to get the dough as close to the shape of a rectangle as you can. Brush the dough with the melted butter and sprinkle with the cardamom and sugar, if using. Roll each piece of dough up. Line 2 sheet pans with parchment paper. Move each long piece of dough onto the parchment and wind it into a circle. Cover with plastic wrap and set aside at room temperature 45 minutes.

9 Heat the oven to 350°F.

Continued

10 In a small bowl, whisk together the remaining 1 egg yolk and the cream, forming a glaze. Uncover the sheet pans and brush the top of the dough with the glaze. Place them in the oven and bake for about 25 minutes, until the tops are golden and the bread is cooked through. Remove from the oven and press the king cake baby or dried fava bean into the bottom of the cake if desired.

11 Vigorously mix together the confectioners' sugar, the remaining 3 tablespoons milk, the corn syrup, and the remaining ¼ teaspoon vanilla extract, making the icing.

12 Divide the 3 cups coarse white sugar among 3 resealable plastic bags. Add 4 drops yellow food coloring and 4 drops blue food coloring to 1 bag. Seal and shake until the sugar is green. Add 4 drops red food coloring and 4 drops blue food coloring to the next bag. Seal and shake until the sugar is purple. Add 8 drops yellow food coloring to the final bag. Seal and shake until the sugar is yellow.

13 Smooth the icing over the warm king cake and immediately top with the purple, green, and yellow sugar, alternating the colors as you go around the cake.

14 Slice and serve.

Note: If you don't want to use artificial food coloring, try dyeing the sugar with pureed blueberries, turmeric, and cooked and pureed spinach, after straining the solids from each.

Note: Cardamom is not a traditional king cake flavor, but it is one that I add in mine. If you prefer to omit the cardamom sugar, split each king cake into three equal pieces and roll them out into long strands. Braid them before moving the two cakes onto the sheet pan and fashioning them into circles. Alternatively, fill the cakes with a stuffing of your choice, diced strawberries and crème fraîche or whatever you like.

CALAS

Makes 8 to 10 calas

For years, African-American women sold calas in the French Quarter and Congo Square, crying out, "Calas! Belles calas! Tout chaud!" as they carried baskets full of the piping hot treats on their heads. Some say this act of entrepreneurship was a route to freedom from bondage for some.

Similar to beignets (lighter, flour-based fritters), the cala's richer history, coupled with its dense, creamy interior and crisp, textured shell, makes it so much better.

1 cup medium-grain white rice	¼ teaspoon ground cinnamon
½ teaspoon kosher salt	3 whole large eggs
2½ tablespoons granulated sugar	1 teaspoon vanilla extract
1¼-ounce package active dry yeast	Peanut oil for frying
¼ cup warm water (about the temperature of bath water)	½ cup confectioners' sugar for serving
¼ teaspoon freshly grated nutmeg	

1 In a medium pot over high heat, combine the rice, salt, and 2 cups water. Do not rinse the rice before cooking it: The starch makes the calas creamy. Bring to a boil. Stir once, reduce to low, and cover. Cook 20 minutes. Remove from the heat.

2 Put the rice in a large bowl. Mash it against the inside of the bowl with the back of a wooden spoon, leaving some grains whole to add texture.

Continued

3 In a small bowl, dissolve granulated sugar and yeast in ¼ cup warm water (about 110 degrees). Let the yeast mixture sit until it's foamy, about 15 minutes. Add the sugar-yeast mixture to the rice and stir for 2 minutes. Cover with plastic wrap or a kitchen towel and leave to rise at room temperature overnight.

4 In the bowl of a stand mixer, combine the eggs, vanilla extract, nutmeg, and cinnamon,. On high speed, beat until foamy, 2 minutes. Reduce the speed to low and add the rice-yeast mixture and mix until a loose, textured ball forms.

5 In a large pot over medium-high heat, bring 3 to 4 inches of peanut oil to 375°F (when it's hot enough, a cooked piece of rice should rise to the top and pop).

6 Dip a spoon into the hot oil and then into the batter. Drop a spoonful of batter into the hot oil, letting it roll off the spoon. Fry 3 to 4 calas at a time until golden, about 4 minutes. Using a slotted spoon, transfer to a paper towel–lined plate to drain and cover to keep warm as you finish the rest.

7 Dust calas heavily with the confectioners' sugar and serve.

ACKNOWLEDGMENTS

I'm grateful to everyone who made this book possible, especially the generations of Louisiana cooks who passed down recipes and the stories that go along with them.

I'm especially thankful to my kind husband and partner in everything, Nick DiSalvo, for all the love, support, enthusiasm, dinner parties, and helpful conversations.

Thank you to my precious Clementine, who helped test king cake, tasted countless pralines, and championed my crawfish bread. She is the joy in everything I do.

My sincere gratitude to my dear parents, Jim and Melinda Carter, the smartest, kindest, and most generous people I know. Thanks for teaching me the importance of telling a story and of listening to one too, especially over good food and drink.

To Jim and La, thanks for all the years of cooking, eating, and celebrating together.

To Cathy and Phil DiSalvo, thanks for sharing your vibrant New Orleans family dinners over oyster spaghetti, redfish courtbouillon, and everything else. And for tracking down ideas for rum cake.

To Leslie Jonath of Connected Dots Media, without whom this project would not have been possible. Thanks for your smart suggestions, patient listening, and great ideas.

To my friend Francine Cohen, for introducing me to Leslie and to this project.

To Debbie Berne and Courtney Jentzen of Swiss Cottage Designs, who breathed life into these dishes with their design and illustrations.

Thank you to the team at The Countryman Press, especially editor Róisín Cameron.

To my dear friends, who make all the cooking and eating so much better.

To everyone who loves New Orleans.

Courtney Jentzen would like to thank Carly Martin for her help with the illustrations. Thanks also to Redding, Stevie, and Paul.

INDEX

Absinthe Frappé, 13

Bananas Foster, 70–71
beans
    Jim Core's Gumbo
        Z'herbs, 25–27
    Red Beans and Rice,
        52–53
beef
    Grits and Grillades,
        58–60
    Peacemaker Po-Boy, 36
    Roast Beef Debris
        Po-Boy, 34–35
    Yakamein, 29–31
Bloody Bull, 57
brandy
    Brandy Crusta, 14
    Brandy Milk Punch, 56
bread. *See also* po-boys
    Bread Pudding, 68–69
    Crawfish Bread, 32–33
    Pain Perdu, 64–65

Cake, King, 73–76
Calas, 77–78
chicken
    Chicken and Sausage
        Jambalaya, 45–47
    Chicken in Sauce
        Creole, 42–43
crab
    Crabmeat Ravigote, 17
    Creole Gumbo, 22–24
    New Orleans–Style
        Seafood Boil, 44
crawfish
    Crawfish Bread, 32–33
    Crawfish Étouffée,
        40–41
    New Orleans–Style
        Seafood Boil, 44

drinks
    Absinthe Frappé, 13
    Bloody Bull, 57

Brandy Crusta, 14
Brandy Milk Punch, 56
Hurricane, 16
Ramos Gin Fizz, 15
Sazerac, 12

Eggs Sardou, 61–63
Étouffée, Crawfish, 40–41

French Fry Po-Boy, 35

Gin Fizz, Ramos, 15
greens
    Jim Core's Gumbo
        Z'herbs, 25–27
Grits and Grillades, 58–60
gumbo
    Creole Gumbo, 22–24
    Jim Core's Gumbo
        Z'herbs, 25–27

Hurricane, 16

ice cream
    Bananas Foster, 70–71

Jambalaya, Chicken and
    Sausage, 45–47

King Cake, 73–76

okra
    Creole Gumbo, 22–24
    Smothered Okra, 37
Oyster Stew, 28

Pain Perdu, 64–65
pasta
    Tailgate Shrimp Pasta,
        50–51
    Yakamein, 29–31
pecans
    Pralines, 72
po-boys
    French Fry Po-Boy, 35
    Peacemaker Po-Boy, 36

Roast Beef Debris
    Po-Boy, 34–35
Shrimp Po-Boy, 36
Pudding, Bread, 68–69

Ramos Gin Fizz, 15
Redfish, Blackened,
    48–49
rice
    Calas, 77–78
    Chicken and Sausage
        Jambalaya, 45–47
    Red Beans and Rice,
        52–53
rum
    Bananas Foster, 70–71
    Hurricane, 16
rye whiskey
    Sazerac, 12

sausage
    Chicken and Sausage
        Jambalaya, 45–47
    New Orleans–Style
        Seafood Boil, 44
Sazerac, 12
shrimp
    Creole Gumbo, 22–24
    New Orleans–Style
        Barbecue Shrimp,
        18–19
    New Orleans–Style
        Seafood Boil, 44
    Peacemaker Po-Boy, 36
    Shrimp Po-Boy, 36
    Tailgate Shrimp Pasta,
        50–51
simple syrup, 13

veal
    Grits and Grillades,
        58–60
vodka
    Bloody Bull, 57

Yakamein, 29–31